THE GREATEST JUMP ROPE RHYMES EVER!

ILLUSTRATED BY
GARY LACOSTE

SCHOLASTIC INC.

Based on the book *Jump Rope Rhymes* from Klutz

Copyright © 2019 Scholastic Inc.
All rights reserved.

Illustrations by Gary LaCoste
Design by Lizzy Yoder

ISBN: 978-1-338-35956-5

10 9 8 7 6 5 4 3 2 1   19 20 21 22 23

Printed in China

Just Jumping

These rhymes are good for jumping on your own,
or for jumping with a group if you have a longer rope.

Banana Splits

Banana, banana, banana split
What did you get in arithmetic?
Banana, banana, banana for free
What did you get in geometry?

Birdie, Birdie

Birdie, birdie in the sky,
Why did you do that in my eye?
Birdie, birdie in the sky
Gee, I'm glad that cows don't fly.

Down in the Meadow

Down in the meadow
Where the corn cobs grow,
A grasshopper stepped
On an elephant's toe.
The elephant cried,
With tears in his eyes,
"Why don't you pick on
Someone your own size?"

Miss Lucy

Miss Lucy had a baby,
She named him Tiny Tim.
She put him in the bathtub
To see if he could swim.

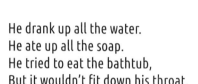

He drank up all the water.
He ate up all the soap.
He tried to eat the bathtub,
But it wouldn't fit down his throat.

Miss Lucy called the doctor.
Miss Lucy called the nurse.
Miss Lucy called the lady
With the alligator purse.

In walked the doctor.
In walked the nurse.
In walked the lady
With the alligator purse.

"Mumps," said the doctor.
"Measles," said the nurse.
"Hungry," said the lady
With the alligator purse.

"Operation," said the doctor.
"Operation," said the nurse.
"Pizza," said the lady
With the alligator purse.

Miss Lucy cont'd.

A quarter for the doctor.
A nickel for the nurse.
A penny for the lady
With the alligator purse.

Out walked the doctor
Out walked the nurse.
Out walked the lady
With the alligator purse.

Miss Mary Mack

Miss Mary Mack, Mack, Mack,
All dressed in black, black, black,
With silver buttons, buttons, buttons,
All down her back, back, back.

She asked her mother, mother, mother,
For fifteen cents, cents, cents.
To see the elephant, elephant, elephant,
Climb up the fence, fence, fence.

He climbed so high, high, high,
He touched the sky, sky, sky,
And he didn't get back, back, back,
'Til the Fourth of July!

On Sunday Night

On Sunday night I lost my dog
And where do you think I found her?
Up on the moon, singing a tune,
With all the stars around her.

Spiders & Bedbugs

I woke up Monday morning
And gazed upon the wall.
The spiders and the bedbugs
Were playing a game of ball.

The score was ten to nothing.
The spiders were ahead.
The bedbugs hit a home run,
And knocked me out of bed!

Five Little Monkeys

Five little monkeys, jumping on the bed.
One fell off and bumped his head.
Mama called the doctor,
And the doctor said,
"No more monkeys jumping on the bed!"

Four little monkeys jumping on the bed.
One fell off and bumped his head.
Mama called the doctor,
And the doctor said,
"No more monkeys jumping on the bed!"

Three little monkeys jumping on the bed
One fell off and bumped his head . . .

(*Repeat the rhyme until you've counted
down to one little monkey.*)

Fortune-Teller

Fortune-teller, fortune-teller,
Please tell me
What do you think
I'm going to be?

Butcher, baker, undertaker,
Tightwad, tailor, bowlegged sailor,
Rock star, painter, cowpoke, thief,
Doctor, lawyer, astronaut, chief.

Ollie Is an Ostrich

Ollie is an ostrich
Who says "O" all day.
Katie is a kangaroo
Who loves to say "K."
When Ollie and Katie
Get together and play,

Everything's always
OK, OK, OK!

I've Got a Dog

I've got a dog,
Her name is Nell,
And what she eats,
I hate to tell:
Tennis balls,
Grandma's shawls,
River stones,
Pork chop bones,
Antique fans,
Rubber bands,
Satin shoes,
Rawhide chews,
If you don't watch out,
She'll eat you, too!

A Horse & A Flea

A horse, a flea, and three blind mice
Sat on a curbstone shooting dice.
The horse, he slipped and fell on the flea.
The flea said, "Whoops! There's a horse on me."

Genius Jumps

These rhymes are a little trickier because you have to think about something else while you're jumping. There are two ways to miss with these games: if you miss your jump, or if you don't get the rhyme right.

Arithmetic

For this rhyme you have to be a good jumper and know your math, too. Jump as long as you can without missing or making a mistake on your math.

Here comes the teacher—
Better think quick!
Now it's time
For arithmetic.
One and one are two
Two and two are four
Three and three are six
Four and four are eight
Five and five are ten

(and so on . . .)

The Alphabet Game

To play this game, you have to fill in the blanks in the rhyme. The first time through, all the words you come up with have to start with the letter A. When you get to the second verse, all of your words have to start with the letter B, and so on all through the alphabet. Keep going until you miss your jump or can't come up with a good word. Whoever gets furthest in the alphabet wins the game.

The rhyme goes like this:

"A" my name is _____.

And my sister's name is _____.

We come from _____

And we sell _____.

This is how you might start out:

"*A*" my name is *Alex*,
And my sister's name is *Alice*.
We come from *Antarctica*,
And we sell *apples*.

"*B*" my name is *Bonnie*,
And my brother's name is *Brendan*.
We come from the *Bahamas*,
And we sell *bananas*!

From Here to There

In this game you have to come up with the names of different places in the world. The first place has to start with the letter A, the second place with the letter B, and so on until you've traveled through the whole alphabet. Keep jumping as long as you can think up a place starting with the next letter of the alphabet.

The first two lines are always the same.
The rest is up to you.
This is one way the song might go:

I took a trip around the world,
And this is where I went:
From *Austin* to *Boston*,
From *Boston* to *Cleveland*,
From *Cleveland* to *Denver*,
From *Denver* to *England* . . .

(*and so on* . . .)

Ipsey Pipsey

After the first four lines of this rhyme, you say the alphabet over and over until you miss. Whichever letter you miss on is the first letter of the name of the person you're going to marry. Really.

Ipsey, pipsey,
Tell me true,
Who shall I
Be married to?
A, B, C . . .

Louie & Lulu

Louie and Lulu are
Twins at the zoo.
A gnu came up and asked,
"Who are you?"
"We're Louie and Lulu,
And twins come in twos."
Two, four, six, eight . . .

(*Count by twos as high as you
can without missing.*)

More Counting Rhymes

Say the rhyme, then try to count as high as
you can without missing.

Red as a raspberry,
Brown as a bean.
That's the prettiest color
I've ever seen.

Yellow as a daisy,
Black as ink.
That's the prettiest color
I do think.

Orange as a pumpkin,
Green as grass
Keep on jumping
As long as you last.
One, two, three . . .

ACHOOOOOO

gesundheit !

Alexander Took a Gander

Alexander took a gander
At a big, green salamander.
He took a big sniff and got a big whiff.
How many sneezes did he sneeze?
One achoo, two achoos, three achoos . . .

Stopped at the Soda Shop

I stopped at the soda shop
On my way home
And now I'm jumping
With an ice cream cone.

Yummy in the tummy
And tasty on the tongue
I won't stop jumpin'
'Til my ice cream's done.

Strawberry, peppermint,
Chocolate chip,
I even like vanilla
With hot fudge dip.

Sprinkles and nuts
And butterscotch goop,
I'll jump with my cone
And count the scoops.
One, two, three . . .

Suitcase, toothbrush,
Going on a jet.
How many souvenirs
Can I get?
One, two, three . . .

When I am a rich girl
I'm gonna be a queen.
I'm gonna have the nicest things
That you've ever seen.
Cars and planes
And a house by lake
How many millions will I make?

One, two, three . . .

Hot Pepper Rhymes

Any counting rhymes can be played as Hot Peppers, but the following rhymes are especially fun. Start out jumping as always. As soon as you come to the end of the rhyme or start counting, jump as fast as you can for as long as you can.

Postman, Postman,
Don't delay!
How many letters
Will you bring today?

Postman, Postman,
Pick up the pace.
Faster, faster,
Let's have a race!
1, 2, 3 . . .

Mabel, Mabel, Set the Table

Mabel, Mabel, set the table,
Just as fast as you are able.
Just be sure you don't forget
Mustard, salt, and Red Hot Pepper!

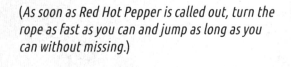

(*As soon as Red Hot Pepper is called out, turn the
rope as fast as you can and jump as long as you
can without missing.*)

wham!

Say, Coach

Say Coach! Hey Coach!
What do you know?
Here comes [jumper's name],
The All-Star Pro.
She can slam it.
She can dunk it.
She's got what it takes.
How many baskets can she make?
One, two, three . . .

Ice cream soda
With a cherry on top
Ginger ale and soda pop.
Keep the rope turning
Until I stop!
One, two, three . . .

Pumpkin, cherry, key lime pie
Drop 'em from an airplane,
and watch 'em fly

One, two, three . . .

Fancy Stuff

These rhymes require that you do a little more than jump. The jumper has to act out whatever the rhyme describes. This works best when you're playing with a long rope and have two people turning the rope, so your hands are free.

The King of France

The king and queen
Came from France
Just to teach me
How to dance.
Jump up high.
(*Jump high.*)
Jump down low.
(*Touch the ground.*)
Clap your hands,
(*Clap*)
And around you go!
(*Turn around.*)

Teddy Bear, Teddy Bear

Pretend to do whatever the Teddy Bear does.

Teddy Bear, Teddy Bear, turn around.
Teddy Bear, Teddy Bear, touch the ground.
Teddy Bear, Teddy Bear, read the news.
Teddy Bear, Teddy Bear, shine your shoes.
Teddy Bear, Teddy Bear, go upstairs.
Teddy Bear, Teddy Bear, say your prayers.
Teddy Bear, Teddy Bear, turn out the light.
Teddy Bear, Teddy Bear, say good night!

(*Jump out.*)

good night!

good night!